"Multimedia artis
a painter, a filmm
to be an original. For that alone, she deserves our admiration... especially since her art is aimed at embracing reality. I must admit that listening to it just once was more engaging than hearing the Top 100 week after week. This collection of poetry and music from Fella Cederbaum is a wonderful full course serving of truths and observations. Instincts tell me that future listenings will inspire new ideas each and every time. After all, asking the tough questions seems so unfashionable these days. But one bold imagination can change all that. So here's to Speech Acrobats, the fuel for the engine on the road to self discovery."

-Greg Victor, Parcbench.live

"I thoroughly enjoyed reading Fella Cederbaum's excellent book of poems [Of Life And Other Such Matters]. She has a wonderful and unusual technique that works very well and seems to me particular to this poet. Her constant questions get the reader involved and make her poems more meaningful, while the subject matter of her work - freedom, Truth and a peaceful existence residing in every one of us - is very interesting. Fella Cederbaum's ability to describe feelings with an interesting use of language lends great depth to her work. I was deeply moved by the almost overwhelming tragedy of Fella Cederbaum's stunning poem What If, [Volume 2] which adds weight to her strong and thought provoking work."

-Mark Wallace, Professor of English (ret),
Thomas College, Waterville, Maine

"Mixing poetry with ambient keyboards, Fella Cederbaum delivers messages of reflection, warning and wisdom like a news editor with a musical heart...."
　　　　　-George W. Harris, JazzWeekly.com

"Fella Cederbaum's powerful poetry [Of Life And Other Such Matters] offers unflinching glimpses into her innermost thoughts and feelings. Written with authenticity, generosity and courage, her compelling musings invite the reader to open the door to their own inner sanctum, creating meaning that stirs the soul and challenges the mind."
　　　　　- Joan Borysenko, Ph.D., New York Times Best Selling author and Keynote Speaker

"While it definitely takes a bit more intellectual attention and patience to experience spoken word poetry set to music than sung lyrics, every, incisive, socially conscious word spoken by the multi-faceted creative expressive Fella Cederbaum on her compelling, ear popping and soul transformative second album Speech Acrobats is worth the investment of time and heart.

The German born daughter of Holocaust survivors, Cederbaum - who starting publishing poetry and fusing her passions for music and poetry in the late 2010s – comes by her hard won wisdom naturally as a lifelong observer taking copious mental notes as she's flourished as deputy director of the Israel Chamber Orchestra, a Boston-based psychotherapist, widely exhibited painter and prolific, highly awarded independent short filmmaker and composer.

Speech Acrobats, which naturally includes her thought provoking cover art, finds the wise sage waxing poetic (literally) about all manner of socio-spiritual issues, finding a genteel, slightly humorous approach to, among other things, take down cancel culture (on the musically whimsical, Latin tinged title track), rap rhapsodically about the easily offended (the bass and synth driven, hip-hop styled "The Great Offense"), question our devotion to our preferred version of the "News" and a pulsating reminder that "Violence" starts at home, "when you're willing to burn cherished friendships on the altar of precious opinions." Yet she's not always biting and negative or in the mood to challenge our devotion to our worldviews.

On the delightful, easily danceable "Truth Tango," she implores us to listen to our hearts and live our lives with joy. Besides the fact that each track has a melodic, harmonic and rhythmic personality of its own (due to Cederbaum's lifetime of skilled musicianship), perhaps the most inspiring aspect of Cederbaum's ventures into music-backed poetry is the way she has distilled a lifetime of thoughts into several minute sound bites worth contemplating a lifetime on."

-Jonathan Widran, JWVibe.com

SPEECH ACROBATS

FELLA CEDERBAUM

This book, or any portion thereof, may not be reproduced in any manner whatsoever without written permission of the publisher except in the case of brief quotations embodied in critical articles and reviews.

Speech Acrobats
Copyright © 2023 MahniVerse Press
MahniVerse Productions™

Cover Art Copyright © 2010 Fella Cederbaum

Cover Art & Design
Fella Cederbaum

FellaCederbaum.com

All Rights Reserved
ISBN: 9798396497221

With greatest love and respect for my parents, whose more than horrific life experiences taught me that not only evil acts, but also silence have consequences and made me first reject, then question everything. I dedicate this book to the one Truth we all share.

"Whenever you find yourself on the side of
the majority, it is time to pause and reflect."
-Mark Twain

"If you would be a real seeker after truth,
it is necessary that at least once in your life you doubt,
as far as possible, all things"
-René Descartes

"The snake which cannot cast its skin has to die. As well the
minds which are prevented from changing their opinions;
they cease to be mind."
-Friedrich Nietzsche

"Truth is incontrovertible,
ignorance can deride it, panic may resent it,
malice may destroy it, but there it is."
-Winston Churchill

CONTENTS

How Do You Know? 1

Experts 7

Truth Tango 11

News 13

Speech Acrobats 19

Violence 23

Don't Talk Nicely 29

Burn My Bed 33

Fear 37

The Great Offense 43

Precious 47

Who? Cares 51

Rip The Bonds 57

Straight-Up Physiology 63

Trigger Tunes 77

Why Are You Running 79

Triggers 83

Without Confirmation 87

Neatly Divided 91

The Prince 93

It's All Your Fault 95

Acknowledgements

About the Author

PREFACE

The majority of the poems in this book were set to music and can be heard on my album *Speech Acrobats*. They mostly constitute the latter part of over two-hundred poetry reflections, which, over the course of several years, have made their appearance spontaneously and unbidden. For most of my life I have questioned the nature of Truth, have pondered the way we construct meaning and reality and what we refer to as mind, the location of which has so far eluded discovery. Questions about love, friendship, suffering, relationship, fear, death, grief, loneliness, God and belief systems. The latter in particular led to a process of inquiry documented in *Speech Acrobats*.

My poems not only continued to initiate themselves as though on their own, but also emerge in the most unlikely circumstances of daily life. They were - and still are - like an irresistible force that unerringly guides me to a place of greater understanding than I was consciously aware of.

Repeated requests for spoken versions of my poems led to the creation of a series of short films set to my music, incorporating some of my paintings and, in my latest short film, featuring *Bambolina And The Doodles*. You can find them, as well as a link to my albums *Truth And Destiny* and *Speech Acrobats* on FellaCederbaum.com as well as on YouTube/@FellaCederbaum.

*"Every word has consequences.
Every silence too."*
-Jean Paul Sartre

SPEECH ACROBATS

FELLA CEDERBAUM

HOW DO YOU KNOW?
August 14, 2021/January 8, 2022

Have you ever asked yourself
How you know what you know?
And what makes you so sure
About the things you know?
Especially when they are
In the field
Of your expertise?

How do you know
That what you know
Is actually correct?
How many
So-called outliers
Can you quietly accept
Before dissonance is reached?
Before your tolerance
Turns ever so slightly
Step by imperceivable step
Turns and turns
Into willful blindness
Which you suppress
Before
You might get alarmed?

And what exactly is it
That might alarm you?
What is so utterly
Threatening

About changing?
Changing a model
That has worked?
A model you hold dear?

What is it
About a model
About the nature of things
And the functioning
Of the world
That can turn
Into a bitter fight
A fight
About wrong or right?
A fight
About position?
Or
Might?

Don't you think
It is more exciting
To seek out
Factual disparities?
Those very discrepancies
That mess up
Your calculations?
Completely challenge
Everyone's conclusions
Your present beliefs?

Yes

Those

The ones that get swept
Under the carpet
The ones
That remain unpublished
Because they don't fit
The prevalent theory?

Isn't it precisely
Those precious
And unresolved problems
That hide
What has been conveniently
Disregarded?
Dismissed?
Maybe even vilified?

A famous cancer hospital
Was known
To develop
Its most innovative treatments
Culled from
What they called
The Book Of Quack Cures
Those cures
Previously ridiculed
Their inventors mocked

Or even
Burned at the stake

But those
Were olden times
We no longer
Tar and feather people
Nor burn them at the stake
That would be too barbaric
For our times
Wouldn't it?

We no longer
Put them in shackles
Nor burn their books
No
We are far more
Civilized than that
We simply allow
For them
To be labeled
Marginalized
Due to those labels

For their voices
To be stilled
Simply cut out
Of the public dialogue
As though
They never existed

And why?
In the service
Of truth of course

However
Wouldn't you agree
That this
Like any truth
Can never be more
Than the truth
Of the moment

And do you know why?
Because tomorrow
There will be
A newer
An even truer
Truth

*****

EXPERTS
January 8, 2022

Have you asked yourself
How so many
With sudden expertise
Appear to be aglow?
Where did all those experts
Come from?
While schools are closed
Teachers don't show

When history is up for grabs
Biographies irrelevant
When language
Grammar
Lost their shape
Destruction deemed benevolent
As long as favourite narratives
Prevail
Are met with blinded zest
And Social Media have free reign
To show you
What is best

Three youngish
Quite robotic men
Control our world
Of knowledge
Determine who is right
Or wrong

And silence some
Abolish
What does not fit
Their personal views
Nor those
Of their dominions

No more pretense
Who needs free speech
The goal is one opinion
That can be managed
From above

Banish biology
And math
Sheer benevolence at work
Prescribes the one
And only path

Some words are in
Many are out
To fit our current times
Tradition
Is racist
So are you
Meaning is changing
On a dime

But who needs meaning
When you can use
Some buzzword

Thick as mud
As long as you
Will follow rules
Defend them to the blood

Adapt
Fit in
Believe the things you're told
There is no place
For the 'Deplorables'
Who obviously have sold
Their little minds
To wrong beliefs
That have been
Long outdated

Time to wake up
To Brave New World
For group-speak
We are slated

*****

TRUTH TANGO
May 29, 2021

Our world is in disarray
It is the price you pay
For not pursuing Truth's
Divine Communion

The world is here to stay
Who cares what people say
Just listen to your heart
Forget opinions

Let Truth show you the way
Stay loving come what may
Detect and banish lies
And their dominions

Abandon taking sides
Instead let's all unite
We've seen there is no gain
In war conscription

Look up into the sky
Allow your heart to fly
Embrace this life with joy
That's my prescription

Remember
There's only one Truth
The truth
You have known from youth

Embedded deep in your heart
Much better than media gazing

No need to watch the news
Get out your dancing shoes
Let's sing
Unleash our voice
With hearts ablazing

Take off your mask and smile
Let's celebrate in style
Remember who you are
You are amazing

*****

#
January 6, 2022

For those of you
Who always know
What's true
Who trust
What you ingest
And never question
What you see
Believe
Your News
Withstands all tests

I first of all
Must ask you this
Does not
The very thing
Called News
Defy that there are many?
How otherwise
Are stories
From the News
Any different
From the stories
Told by Granny?

But
If you do believe
All News is relative
I want to ask again

How can you be sure
I mean
If there are many News
How can you tell
The more secure?

Is it the one
That never lies?
Its reports
Firmly reliable
Makes utter sense
To you
Consequently
Undeniable?

Presents you
With what fits the known
At least in your surrounding
And as you know
There is a slew
Of endless sources
Though to you
Those might be
Quite confounding

The "other" News
Just must be wrong
Because you are
Oblivious
But
As you say

You made your choice
Regard the rest
Insidious

I say oblivious
Not to insult
Rather to state
What you have told
That you prefer
Not hearing that
Which does not match
Your fold

How is it though
You can be sure
When hardly anyone
These days
Goes out
Investigates
For herself
Before her
Latest news
Is aired
Into the world
Of preferential channels?
Broadcasters telling you
Their facts
Dictated by
Their policy panels

A picture

Speaks a thousand words
That
Is a well-known fact
Yet pictures' angles
More than one
Required to be correct
Not merely one
To fit some narrative
Would be essential here
There are so many narratives
Including those
You fear

If there are things
You never heard
Nor ever saw them written
If your News
Simply omitted them
How can you know
What's hidden?
Unable to make choices
While unaware of a design
Was there intention in the mix?
Or was it all Divine?

A single source
Distributing
A storyline to all
And those who dare not follow it
Are destined to be called
Some names

Pejoratives
Or be dismissed
At best
No matter if events
Occurred
That changed the world
At whose behest?

How do you trust
Your sources then
What gives you
Your convictions
Allows you
To defend your views
Without some bad infliction?

Not onto others
But yourself
Cause ignorance
Will reign
Sadly supported
By resisting
Some deep and inner pains

Those inner pains
That are in place
To garner
Your attention
To what is yearning
Deep inside

From realms beyond
Our comprehension

Those inner pains
That are in place
To garner
Your attention
To what is yearning
Deep inside
From realms beyond
Consension

*****

SPEECH ACROBATS
April 9, 2022

This is for you
And that is for I
I have heard
It is time
To bid language
Good bye

You can say
What you wants
Talk gently
Or grunt
It is impact
That counts
Your intent
Pure affront

Them is
Cis gender
And they is
A man
Them bearded
Birthers
Is pregnant
Again

They speaks
Them's language
Understanding?

Your game
Don't other me
Stupid
We is all
The same

Phenomena
Singular
Phenomenon
What?
Nu-cu-lar?
Families?
I have
My rat

Don't mention
Colour
Nor lame
Nor fat
We is
Shades of grey
Speech acrobats

Rename
With abandon
To suit
Every whim
Enlightening
Young children
With sex
Is

Full in

Best when
They are young
Before brains
Fully formed
No common
Sense
A brand-new
Norm

I thinks
What them says
You do
What I wants
Or we'll cancel
Your Facebook
And Twitter
Accounts

Now you knows
You is dead
"Cause you vanish
From view
That is
The idea

You gullible
Fool

*****

VIOLENCE
February 27, 2021

Violence starts at home
Violence starts
When you are willing
To burn cherished friendships
On the altar of precious opinions

Violence starts
When you shut out
And silence those
Who happen not to inhabit
The machinations
Of your mind
Of your convictions
Of your articles of faith

Violence starts
When you prefer to look
For the grand oppressor
Out there
While the petty tyrant
Inhabiting your heart
Whispers in your ear
Whispers and whispers
Incessantly
Until you believe
His utterings
Believe them to be
The voice of reason

Or
The voice of love
Or
Even the voice
Of your very own heart

And that is
The point of no return
When justifications rise
Rise to still
The remaining stirrings
Of your conscience
While offering up
Your true north
To the self-righteously
Indignant
To the self-righteously
Outraged
To the self-righteously
Wronged
The self-righteously
Deeply wronged
Utterly offended
By those
Who would dare
Follow the dictates
Of their own heart

Their own heart
Open
Open by its very nature

Open to listen
Open
To give
The previously unthinkable
The benefit of consideration
The benefit of the doubt
The benefit of validity
When offered
By those dear to them
Or
When offered by wise men
Even
If not of their own conviction

And thus those voices
Those voices
Other than your own
Are stilled
Are cancelled
With Machiavellian fervour
Those other voices
Ideas and experiences
Are silenced
Burned on the altar
Of expedient censorship
Burned like the ideas
The art
And the music
Of
The Other
Burned

Like the undesirable books
Of last century
Burned
As a prelude
To the burning of Jews
A prelude
To the burning of Gypsies
A prelude
To the burning of Gays

A mere prelude
To the burning
Of
The Deplorables

Yet
In allowing the vilification
And the glorified burning
Of the inconvenient
You too are removed
Removed
From the wonders
Hidden in the caverns
Of your mind
The true wonders
Only revealed when you allow
The unfamiliar
The unknown
That which has not been
Incessantly regurgitated
And that which is other

Than tepidly digested news
Proffered up as Truth

In allowing this vilification
Of
The Other
You are removed
From the doorways
To mysteries
Hidden underneath
Every single storyline
Of Truth
Hidden underneath
The place-keeper
Of all that is waiting
To be
Discovered

*****

DON'T TALK NICELY
January 4, 2022

Don't talk nicely
While keeping trash
Behind your tongue
Don't smile at me
When we are face to face
With inner eyes quite numb

Don't say you love me
While you call me names
Not to my face
But behind remains
Of the things you thought
Just before we spoke
Eye-roll
Disparaging
Don't you think
I recognize the note?

The note
That rings
Through everything
You say
And then you look at me
With barely veiled
Disdain
Complete dismay
That once again
Things turned out differently

Than planned
Don't you know
They always do
Unless
You perform the dance?

The ritual dance
Of families
Or different gatherings of sorts
So let me tell you
Participation
In this social sport
Has ceased to tempt me
Long ago

I'll leave my jewelry at home
Just like those shoulds
And shouldn'ts
Considered proper social form
I won't be rude
Nor will I hurt you
Purposely
However
Being who I am
Is not negotiable
Whether brilliant
Dumb
Or clever

You are welcome
Any time

To try
If you can tolerate me
As I am
With my own thoughts
Conclusions
And Ideas
Would love to share them
If I can

Am always interested
To find what's true
And know the source
Of endless difference
To understand
The reasons
Why thoughtless loud
Belligerence
Leads dialogue these days
With willful blindness
Quite ignorant
Of what could set us all
Ablaze

I simply want to find
Where I'm mistaken
Or
Have gone astray
But please
Don't judge me
Just because I say
And think

And feel
Quite differently
From you
Different from all your friends

So what?

Who says that many people
Always own
The one and only truth?
They either do

Or not

Maybe one lonely man
Will prove to know
What is right
The earth no longer flat
In spite perceptions
Concepts
Or ideas
You formulate
By sight

Remember
Galileo's plight

*****

BURN MY BED
Woodmere, July 19, 2017

The story unravels
Illusion is dead
Drown my computer
Burn my bed

My heart is crumbling
This time for good
No need to tell me
The things I should
Or should not do
If clever
In this life or ever
It's not about doing
It's more like the weather

The dream unravels
Illusion is dead
Destroy my piano
Burn my bed

No need to admonish
Your friend or foe
When hearts truly soar
There is nowhere to go
There is simply no question
Of making decisions
Love guides your actions
With surgeon's precision

The plot unravels
The story is dead
Shred my dance shoes
Burn my bed

All linen is tainted
The heart rebels
As untamed spirits
Will surely be felled
By the depth of a truth
Tucked away and hidden
Now it revealed
Its face
Completely unbidden

Smash my buddhas
Destroy mirrors as well
Tear up my photos
Unleash all hell
All laughter
Extinguished
All smiles are dead
All dreams
Down the drain
Burn my bed

No hope for the future
For things to change
Remember that only
God can arrange
How life shows up

For better or worse
Whatever you do
You'll end up
In a hearse

Illusion unravels
The dream is dead
Destroy MahnoDahno
Burn my bed
Rip up my poems
Have all sparkles chopped
Burn paintings and songs
All music
Has stopped

*****

FEAR
January 11, 2013/August 7, 2015

Today I want to ask you
What you know about fear
I mean the kind of fear
That grips you
Not only
In the pit of your stomach
But retracts your vocal cords
So it seems
That sound
Cannot possibly
Vibrate their fibers
Ever again

I mean
The kind of fear
That stops your breath
From reaching any further
Than the bottom of your tongue
Where it meets that choking lump
That settled there
Quite unbeknownst to you

I mean
The kind of fear
The mere thought of which
Has you willing
To trade your life
In exchange

For not having to face
That fear
Ever again

And not the kind of fear
That tends to arise
When faced
With a dangerous situation
Or
The fears of childhood
When many things are ominous
And overwhelming
By definition
Because you were small
And defenseless

And to be quite sure
That you know
Which fear I mean
It is the one
That is bottomless
Endless
And worst of all
Nameless
Which is
Why there is no escaping it
Or
So it seems

I want to ask you
What you really know

About this terrorist of a feeling
This collection
Of unbearable sensations
And overpowering thoughts
That can completely darken your life
In less
Than an instant

Have you ever asked yourself
What brought this into existence?
What propelled it into your path?
And why?

Have you ever tried
To challenge this fear?
Stare it down?
Call its bluff?
Or
Be curious
What it wants of you?
Observed what makes it stop?

And I don't mean pretending
That it was never there
Like whistling in the dark
But rather
Inviting it
To show all of itself

Offer up your blood
As to sharks

Surrender?
As you would in battle
When all is lost for sure?
Lift up your arms
And walk
Towards your enemy?

Trust me
You are equipped
To make it through
And
In a flash so bright
With swift and lightening cut
Manjushri's sword appears
With fiercest might
Returns to you
With wisdom's light
The peace of mind you earned
By not avoiding truth

By not avoiding truth
Nor
Strike defensive postures
Hiding
Behind some story lines
Creating new contractures
With newfound strength
You start to see
That fear is merely that
Which opens up the door to realms
You had not travelled yet

Like everything that lies beyond
The facts you have ingested
Beyond the things you learned in life
That have you so invested
To keep at bay
What you dislike
Ignore
Those long-sown seeds
Try to control
The flow of fate
Arranged
To suit your needs?

Doesn't that just make you laugh?
Because you know
It's true?
So next time fear appears
Simply remember
It is not made of glue
But rather
A configuration thing
A choice of mind
For certain

Fear merely hides
Inside itself
Like thickest
Velvet
Curtain
A treasure trove of openings
To doorways so divine

To that
Which you can never find
While you protect your mind

So you can see
Fear is your friend
Your heart's
True calibration
Unabated
It is your deepest call
Doorway
To liberation

*****

THE GREAT OFFENSE
January 11, 2022

How do you know
What you know
But don't know
What you don't
Yet you think
What you know
Is enough

How do you make
Up your mind
From the news
So opined
Social Media
Accounts
Full of stuff

Full of stuff
That you hate
Or you love
Or berate
Yet hearing
The truth
Is too tough

For the triggered
And frail
Who go straight
Off the rail

Hear an innocent word
Great offense
Just an
Innocent word
Or a pronoun
They heard
Is a call
Take up arms
And defend

How do you say
What you say
Yet don't say
What you don't
Can you say
What you say
Is correct?

How do you know
When you said
What you said
If you said
The unknown
Neither said
Nor fact-checked

How do you call
People names
Without any shame
But expect only
Love and respect

Why would those
You despise
Even wish their demise
Yet believe
You and yours
Are perfect

Why do
Them he and hers
Want the world
To defer
To the half percent's
Rights and insist
That all women
And men
State their pronouns
For them
This entitlement leads to
Blacklist

How do you think
This will go
If nobody knows
And knowledge
Is racist domain
Who can know
What is right
When the loudest
Decide
And tweets are their

Claim to fame

When the news
Is from Twitter
Offended constantly bitter
How the world
Has left them behind
Can you see
How this ends
When what's normal
Is bent
Our world
Is in deadly decline

Can you tell me
Oh Lord
Can you show me
The door
To get off
This upside down
Earth
I'm confused
By the times
That turned
On a dime
Now I pray
For no more
Rebirth

*****

PRECIOUS
January 11, 2022

Today
I am intensely
Curious
Have been wondering
Why
Lately
Even innocent questions
Are often dismissed
As spurious

How could questions
You hear
Be enough
To rouse some fury?
How could they instantly
Call up
An inner jury?

Have you ever wondered
What it is
That makes
Your beliefs
So dear to you?
So precious
That there is no way
To see
If maybe
There is something new?

Maybe something
Of importance?
Or maybe
A smallish detail in the mix?
Could certain views
Be incomplete
If some ingredients
Were missed
In the conclusions
You have drawn?
Or
That were based
On a faulty source?
Yet
You still defended them
With greatest force?

What is it
That makes convictions reign
In service of your defense?
Not in your defense to me
But rather
Inside yourself?

Why
Would you insist
To adhere
To your beliefs?

Could there be more
Than meets the eye?
And why

Would that be
Offending?
What place in you
Is it
That is so attached?
To what exactly?

Can you explain allegiance
To what you heard
Rather than
To what is new?
And why are you
Convinced
This should be
A source
Of grievance?

I would so love
To understand
Why it is deemed OK
To dismiss?
Completely ignore voices
Just because they are other
Than your own?

Why is it so impossible
To simply jump
Into the fray?

Into the fray
Where all of us

Engage in dialogue?
Check out those things
We did not know
And fill in gaps
Where heretofore
There have been
Many
Cover-ups?

Remember
Cover-ups might remove
Certain things from view
But that is all
The truth beneath
Remains
Forever in the brew
The brew cooked up
By our collective minds

Don't you think
It would be best
To include
Both?

Yours?
And
Mine?

*****

WHO? CARES
July 10, 2020

Main Stream Media is corrupt
Never mentions what is really up
Google governs us
There is Twitter news
Fox reports selective truth

Festival new name for riots
Plunders
What of all those great
Demented blunders
Have you purged
Your Facebook posts of late
Before they'll find
Your high school blackface date

Environment completely wrecked
Coal mining
Fracking
Won't be back
Blacks hate Whites
And both hate Jews
White Supremacists hate all
But few

Our language
Has been taken hostage
Safe spaces
For the fact-accosted

Words and thoughts
So dangerous
Oh dear
Quite haunted by imagined fears

WHO CARES

Covid virus going wild and crazy
Vaccination mandates for the Navy
W.H.O. still running China's virus story
Iran regained its long-lost glory

Menstruators found in women's loos
Trans-women cutting off their boobs
Nuclear deal is distant past
Abortions fashionably cast

White males toxic
And they should be banned
Trans men in woman's sports
A winning brand
Gone With The Wind
Has lost its cool
Re-written histories for fools

Trillion dollar mega-deficit
Inflation giving us a fit
Amazon is so much better off
Economy disaster sloth

WHO CARES

Historic monuments
Heads off
Destroyed
You know who is overjoyed
Plural pronouns
Are now used for singles
Black Jesus latest PC symbol

Endless booster shots
Then microchipped
Bill Gates is funding
Testing strips
Brothers Big Tech
Skewing all elections
Facebook censors right-wing
Ad selections

Are you properly insulted now
Have I poked
Your favourite peeves?
Are you outraged?
Up in arms?
Were your weaknesses unpeeled?

Is your ego hurt and bruised?
Were your wishes ruined
And derailed?
That's the whole idea
My friends
Remember
Truth can not be felled

Have you asked yourself
Who it is who cares
Little brain-bound mind
That dares
To appropriate the world
With its selfish tiny human swirls

As though originator of all things
Self-righteously owning happenings
You can never call your own
There's no peace in that
Now go and stay at home

WHO? CARES

'Cause at bottom line
You have no say
Remember you can never sway
How life unfolds on its own terms
It includes disease and germs

It includes the full nine yards
Of all you hate
Or fear
Or love
So stop thinking things are wrong
Or right
Just surrender to life's might
Events will come and go forever
Pleasure
Pain

And those you'd rather sever
Just get on board
God paid your fare
Now exclaim full heartedly

WHO CARES

*****

RIP THE BONDS
November 1, 2011

Rip the bonds
Of all conceptual structures
Those labels
Cause the heart to fracture
Flee from the concepts
Of tiny vision
Of body parts and cell division
Flee to oblivion from those things
They just inflate all suffering

Fly free
That is the motto now
Fly free
And don't you ever bow
Don't even bow
To dedicated teachers
And don't hold wisdom's
Truest features

Don't hold Truth
That is not yours
Don't hold on
And don't endure
Throw out the words
But keep the teachings
And pay attention
No more reaching
For attainments' glow

Or Realization
And give up all your Dedication

Now look closely
Can you see?

Exactly

Now
My Love
You are
Free

*****

*"Don't bend; don't water it down;
don't try to make it logical;
don't edit your own soul according to the fashion.
Rather, follow your most intense obsessions mercilessly."*
-Franz Kafka

THE OVERLOOKED

STRAIGHT-UP PHYSIOLOGY
July 14, 2018

Cautionary Note: For those of you who might take offense at my usage of purely anatomical terms, please feel free to substitute your preferred designation of the body parts in question

Lately I have been pondering
The question of certain public spaces
And the various populations
Deemed suitable
Or
Unsuitable for them
I am wondering
If you too
Have thought about
The nature of your gender?
What it means to you
And what makes you
Identify with one?
Versus the other?
Irrespective
Of your existing
Biological structures
Especially those of you
Who feel
They landed
In the wrong body?

I am wondering
Whether you happen to remember
When this unfortunate incident

Actually happened?
Which part of you exactly was it
That took the wrong trajectory?
And where did it come from?
And how?
When did you first recognize
Those feelings?
How did you distinguish them
From other feelings
You might have had
Of
For example
Dissatisfaction or discomfort
In your own skin?

Did those feelings
Stay with you
The way they first arose?
Or did they
Give rise to thoughts
That guided you?
To experience yourself
In that particular way

To self identify
As being distinctly different
From your genetic
And readily observable self?
Maybe guided you
In the same way
As you would later

Self-identify
As you might
As an accountant?
Or maybe as a
Kindergarten teacher?
Versus
A high-school professor?

Or maybe
You always had those feelings
But never thought about them
Until a particular moment in time?
And of course
I would love to know
About that very moment
When this surprise
Revealed itself to you

And I am also wondering
About the whereabouts
Of those feelings
Or thoughts
Associated with them
Before you discovered
That you were living
Inside the wrong body?
Where were those feelings housed?

And here my next question is
Which body?
Was it your body

When you were maybe
Ten years old?
Or maybe five?
Or seventeen?

The thing is
I honestly don't understand
The nature of
The obvious degree
Of you misery
That seems to
Propel you
To your actions
And I truly don't care
What particular gender you are
Nor about your desires
For new anatomical configurations
Nor do I feel
I need to be involved in
How you choose
To see yourself
Or others
In terms of their body
In terms of their preference
Whether gorgeous
Or shoddy

I am not
Overwhelmingly interested in
How you sleep
With whom

Or with what
I would rather know
What drives your thoughts
Drives your cravings
Compels you
To rearrange yourself
Would like to know
What makes you decide
You need to change
Your basic biology
Rather than be exactly who
And how you are
Exactly the way
Life happened
To have made you
Just like it made
Everyone else

Well
Maybe I can understand a little bit
What you feel
Because
When I was young
I had a strong desire too
Possibly even similar to yours
Actually
At times
Even when I was older
And found myself
In the middle of nowhere
On a hike

Or maybe on a beach
I so wished
For a little penis
An attachment to allow me
To follow nature's call effortlessly
Less vulnerable and exposed
So convenient

Of course
There were other desires too

So What

Do you really think
That a world can be designed
To heed 8 billion individual desires
Of varying shades and inclinations
To follow the specific wishes
Or whims
Of each of them?
Lest a cry of outrage
A cry of discrimination
Of the disenfranchised self-identifiers
Gives hives
To the politically correct?

To not only heed 8 billion
Individual desires
But to change the entire world
According to the whims
Of a tiny minority?

Please know
I fully support you
Support
Your quest for happiness
But do you truly think
Your happiness hinges
On an urgent necessity
For political debate
About the details
Of how you happen to wish
To fulfill your bathroom urges?
Or
Of how your needs
To be viewed
While inside bathroom facilities
Or locker rooms
For that matter
Get met?
Especially when your claims
Do not match
Your obvious biological appearance

Do you truly believe
That how you desire
To change your physiology
Whether symbolically
Or
In actuality
Should take a major place
In the public arena?

Do you really think anyone
But you
Should be interested
Whether you would like
To acquire new body parts
Or
Whether your penis
Or any other aspects
Of your physiology
Offend you so much
That you feel compelled
To have them refashioned
Or cut off?

Why not simply go ahead
And do
What you must?
But why is it
You think you need to involve
The entire world
In such an extremely private affair

And apart from that
Please
Do not inflict the consequences
Of your personal entitlement
On those of us
Who do not presently own a penis
And are not in the least interested
In changing this condition
Whether convenient or not

Do not inflict
Your personal preference
Your insistence
To use your penis
In public places
Where those without one
Have to follow your visit
And deal with the
Consequences

And please
Before you run off with a pout
Or feel offended
Or misunderstood
I do have a great solution
For all of us
A very simple one
To end this particular debate
Once and for all

It is the establishment
Of
Physiology Bathrooms
Exceptionally easy
And certainly most cost-effective
I would like to make a pitch
For new bathroom
And locker-room signage
The labels can read
In two ways only
Based on

Two perfectly clear situations
Based on
Straight-up physiology
And
Even better
Easily self-identifiable
Two options only
The image of a penis
Or a crossed out penis
Or
As a concession to those
Who vociferously object to the latter
It could be
Any other image
To denote the absence
Of an outer urination protrusion

And who really cares
Who might be the owner
Of any such
Urination appendage
Whether mixed
Male
Female
Or any combination thereof

However
I do care if humans
Born with male bodies
With male chromosomes
Especially those

Who went through
The hormonal changes
Of puberty
Want to compete
In women's sports
And
With their larger
And more muscular bodies
Larger hearts
And greater lung capacity
Instantaneously displace
All those humans
Who never were endowed
With those same
Physiological advantages
That was
After all
The whole reason
For establishing
Separate sports leagues

Separate sports leagues
To afford those humans
With biologically female bodies
Opportunities to shine
In their own right

Therefore I suggest
A wonderful
Very special
Less confusing new league

Of
Trans Identifier Teams
Rather than
Completely destroying
Competitive sports
For all biological women
Who neither crave
To be de-womanized
Nor to be completely
Re-classified
In order not to offend
The newly gendered humans
In their midst

While I don't care
Whether you feel
You were born
In the wrong body
Nor what gender you are
Nor what gender you choose
I expect you to afford
The same respect to women
Biological women
As you demand from them

The same respect
For their wishes and needs
Without being forced to cater
To newly fashioned
Female derivatives
In their midst

And remain to be women
In the same way
They always were

I heard it said
That happiness
Is an inside job
However
If you do believe
Changing your gender
And its visible indicators
Will make you happy
If you believe
That changing on the outside
What disturbs you from the inside
Will make you happy
Please
Go ahead

And I hope
You will not have
To change your mind
And I hope
You will not expect me
To be responsible
Neither for your fateful cut
Nor
For any re-attachment procedures
Nor for the demolition
Of already existing
Perfectly suitable bathrooms

Perfectly suitable for all those
Who are willing to tolerate
Their perfectly
Or
Imperfectly functioning
First edition body parts
Rather than equip themselves
With bad imitations
Of their inner cravings
Because
I truly don't care
Which combination of biology
You feel chose you
Nor what gender you are

The truth is
That I am interested in
Equal rights
For all members
Of the human species
In all its colours and shades
In all shapes

With or without
Their appendages

*****

TRIGGER TUNES
January 4, 2021

I am sensitive
To many things
Would you please
Pay more attention
Stop saying
Your offensive words
You give me hypertension

REFRAIN
I get triggered by stupidity
There is nothing I can do
It makes my brain
Spin like a storm
Anxiety engulfs me too

The thought of water
Makes me gasp
And please
Don't mention rain
Our kitten drowned
When I was eight
And I was beaten
Blamed

REFRAIN

Show me the safe spaces here
Someone just asked for money
Can't they recognize my trauma
I grew up
Poor and hungry

REFRAIN

Stop calling people Black or White
Find both words so traumatic
I am half and half and colour-blind
Need protection from semantics

REFRAIN

Did someone here utter "man" again
That terrifying reminder
One looked at me the other day
Fluid people are much kinder

REFRAIN
I get triggered by stupidity
There is nothing I can do
It makes my brain
Spin like a storm
Anxiety engulfs me too

*****

WHY ARE YOU RUNNING
February 28, 2021

When I was young
We delighted
In asking the question
Do you know
What is mean?
And the answer
We all delighted to give?
Mean is
To push someone
Down the stairs
And then ask them
Why are you running so fast?

It was hilarious
Or
So we thought
Yet today
No question is posed
As to the mysterious disappearance
Of dissenting voices
As to the consequences
Of silencing voices
By first pushing them aside
To the margins
Of the visible
To the outer limits
Of the audible
The question asked today

And in the same breath
As decrying the inconvenient
And upon discovering
The reappearance
Of those silenced

Their reappearance
Independent of the dictates
Of official narratives
Their authenticity is mocked
Their validity
Contemptuously dismissed
Due to their appearance
Yes
That's right
Their appearance
In the invisible margins

Those very same margins
Into which they had been
Forcefully expelled
Manipulated
Under some smug guise
Of benevolent intentions

Free speech
For the chosen
Free speech
For the self-appointed judges
Of the acceptable
Acceptable

And therefore true
Because they say so
And what is more
They agree
The choir of the converted
Speaking in one single voice
Solidified by consensus bias

How convenient

*****

TRIGGERS
January 5, 2022

My friend Marie
She asked me
What on earth
Just triggered THAT?
Well
Every poem has a trigger
Every poem has a cause
But who knows
What causes really are
What is their real source

You could say
A mood was cause
Gave rise so some reflection
But then I ask you
What's the reason
For your mood?
What triggered its reaction?
Was it your family?
Or your spouse?
That left you in a fog?
Or did your cat
Get sick?
Or did you lose
Your dog?

It left you
In a royal funk

A broken heart?
A rage?
Now can you tell me
Why you acted thus
And not some other way?
What is the cause
Of how you are
What holds you
In its sway?
So let me ask you
How it is
That you never
Had a horse?
When I was young
We had a bird
He flew away
Of course

Do you think
I am straying
From the question asked
What was the trigger?
I could continue
On and on
The story
Ever bigger
Unendingly
Revealing causes
That lie
Behind some others
From the start

We might as well
Go to time zero
When was that?
You ask me
You are smart

You tell me
What came first
I mean
The one and only trigger
That things are this
Rather than that
Now it's up to you
To search
With rigor
Without concession
Whatsoever
To indulgent speculation

You'll see
What happens next
I predict
Some serious
Elation

*****

WITHOUT CONFIRMATION
January 5, 2022

Do you know
Who you are
Without confirmation
From others?
Without reflections
You see in the eyes
Of loved ones?
Your children?
Your sisters?
Your brothers?

Do you know
Who you are
If there is no one
Who knows
What you accomplished?
How you look
In your soul?
If no one remembered
Neither courage
Nor fame
Nor the status
You like to hold?

Do you know
Who you are
When no one shares
The beliefs

You hold so dear?
Those ideas and concepts
Those opinions of yours?
Your convictions
Whose loss
You so fear?

Do you know
What to do
When no one
Around
Agrees with you
Nor is interested
In what you think?
Does not share
Your views?

Have you wondered
Why
Like crazy glue
You adhere
To what you already know?
Why there is no place
For something new
Does it threaten
To change you?
Maybe
Make you grow?
Maybe stumble at first
When haltingly
You explore the unknown?

Could exhilaration
Then quicken your stride
As you notice
You have wings?
Wings
Of your own?

Wings
That were hidden away
By some crusty beliefs
Maybe habits
So hard to shake
Did you know
You had wings?
Quite ready to go?
Once you give up
Having your cake?
Yes
Having your cake
And eating it too?
Wanting freedom
Yet hang on to prison?

Your wings are here
To deliver you safely
Leave behind
This kingdom
Driven by fear

*****

NEATLY DIVIDED
2-23-22

Did you always think
Just like I did
That not only countries
Were neatly divided
But things and places too
That everything
Had a clear circumference
Or a boundary
Like a foot
Is not a shoe
And Germany
Is not Belgium
Nor is Poland
Brazil
That skin is
Where your body ends
And ….

So is everything
Just one big soup
Intermingled in degrees

Yet
When you look at atoms
Or
Quarks

Can you tell

**The end
Of your dog's bark??**

*****

THE PRINCE
6-7-22

She said
I thought
You were a prince!
Don't you kiss
Frogesses any longer?

Not me
And
Please know
I no longer
Kiss
Narcoleptic ladies either

And for that matter
Please go
And fight your own dragons
Since trans princesses
Don't fight for
Cisses in distress

We
Have the fastest
Spinning Wheels

*****

IT'S ALL YOUR FAULT
Song For The Perpetually Guilty
October 1, 2022

Here I have a crazy question
For the guilt-plagued souls
Like you
Who blame yourselves for everything
In your surrounding that's askew

Dabbadumm Dabbadumm
Dabbadumm Dabbadumm
And you believe
It's All Your Fault

When your colleagues feel offended
And your parents are upset
When your neighbours
Are quite crazy
And your children
Lack respect
When your daughter
Goes astray
And your son 's
A sex-offender
While your spouse's crazy driving
Takes him on a fender-bender

When your mother has dementia
And your sugar-daddy is broke
When your uncle joined the mafia

And your brother had a stroke
When your daughter can't get pregnant
And your favourite aunt is delusive
While your youngest is a hooker
Prances naked and seduces
You just know
It's All Your Fault

When your aunt
Is now a man
And her son
Becomes your niece
While your wife
Has changed religion
All she does is
Hug some trees
When your granny
Is your grandpa
And your sister is
Now your brother
While your son
Becomes your daughter
And your father
'S now your mother

Dabbadumm Dabbadumm
Dabbadumm Dabbadumm
And you are sure
It's All Your Fault

When a hurricane rolls in

Wrecks your great remodeled kitchen
Fills your basement
Full of sewage
You should have known
So stop your bitching

When your ex
Takes you to court
And is trying to extort
For no reason
But sheer greed
And she leaves you
In great need
When your father stood
And watched
While his new wife
Threw some knives
At your younger little sisters
And you could not
Change their life

When your partner
Is unfaithful
Screams that
You are the one to blame
Your attempts
To save the marriage
Lead to everlasting shame
When your child is
An alcoholic
Interventions are for naught

And the family is distressed
Never-ending battles fought

Dabbadumm Dabbadumm
Dabbadumm Dabbadumm
Guilty you
Thinks it's All Your Fault

When your feelings
Are offending
And the Truth
Is ever-bending
Your anxiety on the rise
So you will apologize

When your eldest
Is entitled
And your wife goes
Off the rails
You can't make your
Mortgage payments
Cause your new computer
Failed
When your husband
Is abusive
You're afraid to call it quits
And your family endorses
And your life is on the fritz

Dabbadumm Dabbadumm
And you're convinced

It's All Your Fault

But remember
It's like the weather
You can never
Make that better
Your anxiety on the rise
So you still apologize

Are you GOD?
All aglow?
Quite omnipotently know?
It's
ALL YOUR FAULT

*****

ACKNOWLEDGEMENTS

The following acknowledgments are for those, who have, in some form or other, supported, or been directly involved in my creative adventures and the subsequent publication of *Of Life And Other Such Matters, More Other Such Matters* and, specifically this companion book to my recently released album *Speech Acrobats*.

First and foremost, enormous appreciation for my extremely supportive production hero and unbelievably accomplished Photoshop/LogicPro-genius, webmaster, and friend, Steve Catizone, without whom this book would never have seen the light of day, for his huge heart, great ears, versatile expertise - bat-chaser being one of them - and his wicked sense of humour, consistently cracking me up and unfailingly turning the tedious and, at times challenging details of publishing into hilarious occasions.

In equal measure, fondest and most profound appreciation for my incredibly creative genius cinematographer, Bruce Petschek, whose life-long passion for poetry brought him into my life, to magically help birth not only the MahnoDahno short-film series, but who has contributed his wonderful animation skills to *Speech Acrobats*, featuring *Bambolina And The Doodles*, and who, in that process, has consistently and happily both read and listened to the various iterations of my poems hundreds of times, emphatically encouraging their publication right from the get-go.

With deep respect and unending gratitude to the one and only Song Ahm for everything – known and unknown – and for his miraculous presence in my life.

With gratitude for all my teachers, especially the unwitting ones.

To my sweet, very wonderful baby-brother Harry with huge love and enormous appreciation for his unfailing support and for "seeing" my poems and to my dear friend Gloria Greenfield for not only enthusiastically supporting the video versions of earlier poems, insisting on their submittal to film festivals, but who has also given enthusiastic and very much appreciated feedback on *Speech Acrobats* in particular.

Profoundest appreciation for my wild soul-sister, the inimitable painter and "un-teacher" Michele Cassou for her many excited and attentive late-night listens and to my second wild soul-sister, the fabulous pianist Marie Carmichael, for her continued loving feedback on every single one of my creative utterances and for showing up with the most spectacular generosity of heart imaginable.

Very special thanks to my dear friends for always openheartedly and patiently listening to these most recent poems: Ehud Cohen (z"l") Rick and Doreen Leskowitz, Jim and Trish Feijo, Mary Ann Whalen, David Cheng, Tania McNeil, Andrea Sorgato, Misha Yalovenko, Paula Sacks, Bernd Selmeier, Dr. Kristin Foley and my cousin and friend Ellia Nattel-Keren.

Of course, most enormous appreciation goes to my indomitable Yolinka Nash, whose love for my work propelled her to create the poetry corner and feature my poetry on her weekly WABC Radio Show and who now enthusiastically continues to promote *Speech Acrobats*.

And last, but certainly not least, my greatest appreciation to Angelina Logiudice, Vilma Dias and Flavia Martinez for faithfully keeping both looming bureaucratic and home mayhem at bay, allowing me the peace of mind to write.

*****

ABOUT THE AUTHOR

BLAH BLAH BLAH BLAH BLAH BLAH BLAH BLAHBLAH BLAH BLAH BLAH BLAH BLAH

BLAH BLAH BLAH BLAH BLAH BLAH BLAH BLAHBLAH BLAH BLAH BLAH BLAH BLAH BLAH BLAH BLAH BLAH BLAH

BLAH BLAH BLAH BLAH BLAH BLAH BLAH BLAHBLAH BLAH BLAH BLAH BLAH BLAH BLAH BLAH BLAH

Made in United States
North Haven, CT
05 January 2024